I0782379

Remember Me

I am with you………… !

Remember me…………

is all your life story based on fictional

Ways ………

This is a fictional story but…   ! But……!

But you know about it very soon……!

In this book all character are saposed

By sameera khan

Remember Me

I am with you………… !

By sameera khan

By sameera khan

Copyright © [2024]

All rights reserved   No part of this publication may be reproduced, distributed, or transmitted in any form or by any means, including photocopying, recording, or other electronic or mechanical methods, without the prior written permission of the publisher, except in the case of brief quotations embodied in critical reviews and certain other noncommercial uses permitted by copyright law

For permissions requests or inquiries, please contact the publisher at [sameeraartsport@gmail com]

By sameera khan

Remember me

is just a story A fictional horror story is all about the assumed character

The story of a popular writer and a actor of past and future

And a very mysterious life of them past and future and present

And the darkness of there life

But…! You may enjoy it because it is very interesting story of what if you are the nect of this………

Remember Me

I am with you………… !

By sameera khan

The story is began……   !!!!!

"huuuuuuuuu!!!!!!!!!!!!!!!

It was raining heavily that evening, the weather was also quite bad

"Today the weather is so strange, my heart is beating strangely,

Is this what you want to say?

"Why is my heart so sad   ?", what is there to talk about in this day

(She was writing a lot in her diary and then someone rang the bell,

She put her hand on her heart or choked, she was a beautiful 20 year old girl who lived alone in her house

"how are you limna   ?"

(Someone else asked us, there was a girl at the door)

Maybe his friend ho   who knows   )

By sameera khan

"you... what a supriese   ?"

"how are you limna   ?"

(she quickly closed the dairy)

"I am fine   how are you   ?

"Ha! ... i am good

"Or how is your writing going   ?"

"Oh!!! This is moving very badly for me, I don't understand that the climax and I am thinking that now I am written it   a little different   "

"Well Ragni, tell me how everything going "

I will make coffe for you

"You know how big a fan I am of your writing...... ,you know what

Today I also met a woman who was a famous writer   "

"oo   who is she   ?"

"her name is malini shaa"

"what!!!!! you met Malni mam   ho wow

" Yes, but I didn't get her autograph, so I thought I have a very good writer too, my dear Limna, and that's why I thought of you, and I thought I'd go and meet you   "

" You did well   "

"yes

"Or what is going on here   ?"

"every thing is good...   and you know Shekhar wants to expand his business or for this or we are going to sub dubai this time we will meet here

"oh   it's nothing but necessary for success "

"It will be quite difficult to meet again

"I am still there for you "

"you still have to parcel my next book to me "

"yah… I will definitely send it to you" (a strong lightning bolt came from somewhere in the door)

"Haaaaa! How forcefully the voice has sounded, isn't it?

"yes is it

I am very afraid, you live alone in such voices, you are not afraid ?"

" No, why am I afraid? Anyway, wherever I am alone, I have my books with me and we both are happy

"Okay now I have to go "

"ok but come soon   "

"Yes, why don't you contact Malini for the climax of your book… ?

" No, I will write it myself?"

" Yes, but still you can take a help from her, can't you, she's very good anyway, I heard, yes, even though I didn't get her autograph, you're a writer, you're going to get it, right?
"

" No, there is no need, I will think of something myself

(There are many dogs barking outside   )

By sameera khan

"Do you know why people are making so much noise when they are fasting, they are not making so much noise?

Well, this rain is ufff

"No problem, you call the cap

"They had just gone out when the dogs started barking

"There is no point in scolding them so much

"And they are making so much noise

"They say that if the dog starts making a lot of noise, it means that they are seeing ghosts

"What the hell?

"It's a good joke

"Oh no, really

" Limna, … they see ghosts, it's not a joke

"Well, let's see, if it's me and us, then which of us is the ghost

"She is laughing

"Limna   Do you think this is a joke?

"Yah   a very bag joke   she laughed and laughed

"The story of an Atma that too in front of a writer

"Limna listen to me

"Lim

"That's enough ragni   now shut this Ghost story understand

"But

"What but

By sameera khan

"Do you think this time if you say this all i am going to listen you

"But

"What but   ok i accept but now there is only you and me then who is the ghost hear

"Me   she said it with so softly "What nice joke

This is not a joke   limna

"Ooo the it's real   hi hi hi she laughed

"Don't laugh i said you last time

"Ooooo if i laughed then what you do with me

"I   iam   k

"Oooo kill   that's too funny now stop it

"Limna

"What limna

"If you think i am not then ask any one
no one can see me this time accept you

"Look   ragni that's en

"Not now   dear

"Ragni what's wrong with you

"Nothing i am tells you to ask any one
but no one can see me understand

"A   how   h   how that's possible

"Because of anil

"Anil   who is he

"He is the most   important part of my
life

Ragni   before she said she's gone

The rain become more hevey

By sameera khan

Seen 2

Roohi is a psychologist and she is so briliant psychologist   she is very perfect in her work

One day she met the different kind of her one of petient   who is totally different from all

His name is anil

"sister…   !

"yes doctor… "

"You call Anil here

"ok mam

"He was a tall man who looked like a mysterious person

"Look, you're all right now, there's nothing else, and as for these paintings of yours, tell me something about them

"Like what should I tell you?

"That is, by seeing whom you make, you know that printing Often the mind makes our flower making a reality, like your consious mind is responsible for your paintings, but you must have seen it before, so tell me Where did you see it?

"You are a doctor and would know more and as far as the paintings are concerned it is a secret of mine……….

"Yes, but tell me why you are making that painting

"There is a reason, but it is not necessary to tell you

"do not hide anything from the doctor.she said.

"Ooooo really   ?   he laughed

"I have to see those paintings and this is no joke.

"Don't look, doctor.

"But why..

"Why is a good question he laughed like….

"Look, doctor, you seem sensible, and I am telling you not to look, then it will be better for you

"So my wish is that I also want to see the paintings now don't talk much and show me those paintings anyway I am your doctor …….she said with anger.

"Well, I will send it to you in the evening but i warn you .

"Yes

"Hi hi hi   He smiled awkwardly

"He was leaving then, She said to him ."

"ok see you tomorrow.

"We won't see you tomorrow, doctor…"

"Ruhi felt something strange but she didn't say anything to him

"She went straight to her home from the hospital, where she saw a box on her couch

"Jini !!!!!!!!!!!!

  jini !!!!!!!!!!!!!

"Yes mam

"What is in this box and who brought it here

By sameera khan

"Mam this is from anil

"Oooo!!!!!!!

"Yah remember ok you can go …..

"Sent so soon, he said to himself"

he was about to open the box when the phone rang…..

"Ooo who call me this time …?"

"Hello"

"Doctor"

"Yes who speaking"

"Doctor i am Anil's wife   "

"Oooo what happens"

"Doctor anil is no more "

"What !!!!!! !

"What are you saying ?

"Docto   i don't now what happened but before his death he said me

"What

"He said me that I warn you to no see the painting"

"What

"Yes doctor

"Pls don't see the painting that's his last words for you .

"Ooooo , !!!!!!!!!!! omg.

"What   the

"She was sitting on the couch and the book fell out of her hand and she cried, oh my God

By sameera khan

"What happened Anjali?

"Nothing mom i just read my book

"Oh you and your books………

"This is a pretty scary story   I'm doing one thing   I'm going to skip it and the next chapter will be "she told himself

"That's when her mother told her to get up, Anjali, and walk around, why are you sitting with books all day

"Ok mama

, "So she kept her book on table

It was raining very hard outside,

so she wanted me to do something to have fun,

"so he asked his mother to let us get wet"

, so his mother said "Ok, get wet "

Then the phone rang

"Anjali pick up the phone ",her mom said

" ok mom I pick up"

she went there to pick up the phone

" hello…

who is he asked on the phone

" hello

,"Hello "

" you have read"

she was surprised the voice was a bit heavy, she did not understand, she asked who are you, who are you?

"I am anil and you know me…

" listen my voice now I am Anil"

she was scared she thought how can this happen how can a person with a book call hello where are you lost…

" are you listening or not "

She was surprised when anilsaid loudly

"she said how are you in reality ?

"He said it is not necessary to know I have sent a box for you now I am going to receive the parcel don't open this box and look at the letter I said tomorrow an official will meet me"

' She was afraid that how could this happen, only then someone rang the doorbell, she went out there to open the bell, and she saw that there was a person standing with a parcel

And there was a box in his hand that looked like a painting…

"It was a painting, but she didn't open it

He thought he should call her, but he didn't have her number

so he rang him back…

she picked up

" Hello

"you got that painting… ?

Now listen to me, don't open this painting

"Don't look, I'm warn you "

She was scared and closed it back with a woolen khatak

Only then did she see that the same story was happening She was even more scared

Then her mother sHe asked her who is, who is anjili ?

" then she said no one, Mama, my parcel was just the one who came and she went to her room in fear the next day morning

'The next day he got a call back that he called back Anjali

Her So she answered the call say" yes"

then he said "take the painting I sent yesterday and go to coffee mentor"

' and yes Don't worry without this painting …

 She went to the cafe and sat there   There was no one there, but after a while, a strange-looking person sat in front of her and stared at her   He was a tall, strange-looking person

Than he said hello………

Anjali didn't answer her hello,

then he said

"you can't even answer someone's hello"

"I don't answer to unknown people

"Now tell me how you came to know about me and how you really are "

She was surprised It was raining outside It was raining very hard   and it was raining outside he said look

" i know you i know everything i am anil shrivastha "

"What should I do to you? Who are you? How did you know about me? Tell me…   ?

She was very scared at first, but then she chided her loudly

"Give me that parcel, he picked up the box and was about to take it away…

, thens she called from behind, "

" how can you go like this, how are you in reality,……   ?

then he came back to him and sat down and said

"I am anil shrivastha"and I know that you were reading me that book written by me and she was thinking about the book

then he said that book is the story of my life and

she said how   Maybe, but she didn't understand anything

"Look, I don't understand, how can it be in reality? Tell me, how can it be in reality?

" No one can see except you, don't give up loudly that those who will think you are crazy..

She is more surprised and was more worried, was afraid and only …

then he said.." not need to stress the mind more   I wanted my parcel so I get it so good by………

Next seen

"So where are we both going darling…?

" there is a surprise for you

"oh wow surprise then it will be fun

"he removed the blindfold saying this beautiful is your gift oh the best gift you have ever given so

"I liked it very much let'…………… s go inside it was a very beautiful house built by the beach he liked it they both were a married life one was named Priya and the other was named ravi.

"Wow, it is very beautiful from the inside too where is it? Only then, when she said yes, this is your wedding gift, I was not able to give you anything….

Someone was going to bring it here,

Then bell is rang..

Priya said…."is anyone comes…

Ravi…"no ….ok I go to check who is coming…

"there was a strange looking man….a tall and dark but seems some strang personality..

Ravi ask…."who are you……….?

"Look, it is not necessary for you to know my name, but if you are asking, then let me tell you that this house is not good for both of you…   "

" who the hell are you to say this……?

They yelled loudly and.

" he said, "This is Anil's house   Both of you leave here   If you both don't go, he will go It is very dangerous ….

   They were both scared …

" ravi said, "Who are you?"

" Then he said, "I am not the owner of this house "

 Then ravi said, "I am the owner of this house

The strange person said………..''Look, this house can't be yours.''

The priya said.. …….this house is owned by us and you should leave here quickly….

Then   srange   person   said…………that strange person

"If you don't leave here, it will be very bad,
he said so loudly ……….!!!!!!!!!!!!!!!!!

that ravi and Priya got scared

"Look, I am telling you to leave here, it is not
good for you,

 then ravi, we pushed him out loudly and
said, "Get out of here……

then the person said………….."There is a
man's ghost here   His name is anil "

Then fon rang !!!!!!!!!!!!!!

ravi picked up the c

all on his phone after an hour at night and
he

said hello hello……

and he said what the hell I am the owner of this house how can you do this and hung up the phone……

"priya … asked what happened, ?

Then ravi said, "I didn't sign this house, but it became ours   Now at the last minute, the contractor is saying that this house can't be yours, leave here and our deals will be done……

 " They are canceling it and he was getting angry

" Priya said that it's evening,…   something will happen ..

Lets go ravi…..!"

The strange person said…… ”You can't go anywhere from here you both have set the limit and he laughed loudly

“ after laughing loudly …

“he said your mind is getting damaged from everywhere else I will throw you out of this house and he pushed …

' It was only then that the doors of the house were closed and there was darkness everywhere   It was raining heavily outside……

“The rain was falling so hard that …

  Priya didn't understand anything   … that let's run away from here because the door was open, they were about to run away, he said, you couldn't have gone anywhere from here, if you had made a mistake in the house, then who are you, where are you from, then he said, I am anil and this is my house…

You both made mistake in my house and he locked the doors and with that the story ends………

To Be Continue

Next seen

"Press meet, many people, party month, a reporter stood up and he asked malni sha

,I have a question for you   Look,…   this is a very interesting ……….

He ask to become writer what should I do ?

"   She was answering the question very calmly …… And then she said to him,

"Look, to become a writer, you need to understand the character of whatever character you are writing in the story   If you can't understand it, then you can't become a writer   Becoming a writer is not normal "

 If you know how to write, then you are an artist   "

"The second question of love you 7 time   , madam, which is a story written by you, is there going to be a movie about it?

malni said yes

, by the way, I don't think it is good to make a movie about my story on any book, but because of this …..

The director was a very good colleague of mine, so I agreed and a film will be made on it…

then some one else, a reporter asked if a character is going to expand in it ?
" then she saw it and said,

"Well, one story is perfect " There is no need for any character in it but still Mr RK who is the actor for this story wants to expand the story and he wants to expand his character…

"   Because of that they have said yes and there is going to be a movie about it and of course

 you are going to see it very soon but let me tell you that…

"Then he said to another …"You think that no one can become a writer like you, …………..

then malni arrogantly told him

that "yes, no one can't be because to write something and everyone can be a test and I understood

, writing anything on a blank paper is not less than anything.

What do you think? Anyone can become a writer by taking two lines   No, to become a writer, you must understand and anyone can become a writer   He can become a writer only when he has to write something and not everyone can write on everything like………..

Mr   rk…… is also a writer from movie I heard but he is also an actor he is seen more in actors only   We see more in the film industry, but if you are saying that he is an artist and a writer too,

then it is fine to see what he writes…

then she comes to cabin……..

with anger…….

"What the hell is this?

"How come people outside are also asking me ……?

His assistant ask "what happence mam.......?

Then malni see her with anger......

"you asked me what happened......

"then someone knocked on the door and came in …..

He was the r k of a strange but he was quite handsome to look at .

 "He was also an actor and a writer   Even then he said malni.......

" didn't give any answer then he sat down and.

 he said…" as I want to expand this story of yours so you can help me a little bit that's why I have come here malni .

malni said….

" If you don't know, how to write then why change the story…?"

He want to say but malni………

" my story is so perfect that I don't think that you can make it more perfect.

Then r.k said…..''I should add any character in it, so when I don't understand, …

"Then she said,

"Look, I am expanding your role my your story……… Anil will be a very good friend ………"

Even then, malni got angry and said that you are celebrating your nipples, while it was discussed that you are only expanding your role " …

" Now you are talking to me about something else,…

" then he said it loudly   I am also a writer……

Then malni said   "The movie will be bad and your writing is also bad, anyway you can leave here .."

 Manni Shah was so upset at that time that she didn't think it was good to listen to anything "

He said, "Look, you are angry a lot Do you think I am such a writer that I will write anything?"

Then she said, "There is n…

Next seen

"There was a press meet, everyone was gathered there, everyone was talking about the success of this story,…..

 then someone asked…" malni do you think that this big role in your story will make you story perfect?.............. "Has it been or do you think that your story was perfect anyway…………?

" then she said with enough……   "
arrogance ….

"to believe that my story must have been made with a lot of thought and as you can see the success of this movie is fine……   If this character has been expanded in this story………

, someone asked r k……   that do you think that I malni saying to you is right   ?

" r.k said………

"I think that malni is saying absolutely right in this story if any character If he is big then he is good but the story was also very perfect and here ……

, malni and r k saw each other and after a …

And the press is done……

She go after it then r.k …call her pls stop I want to say you something…..

"Malni paused for a moment.

 and then .

"she said, "What do you want to say, r k?"

Then r k said,

 "Look, Mani, I want to say that as the press also asked, I also think that a lot of your story is very important " It was perfect   If you feel bad about me expanding this role, then I want to apologize to you because… .

"So on my side, there are many roles, but there is a lack of a friend in it, but still it was a story   I want to apologize to you   You know what I have done...

she said, "Look, you must think that you have proved yourself brilliant by writing this......

" I am not saying that you are not a writer, but to become a writer, it is not necessary to be an expert in a story, but to understand the story " Whatever your story told in this film, my story was a hit and so was yours......

"So it doesn't matter whose story was a hit, the movie was one, what else is needed, whatever it is, both were right and both were not wrong...

If you are a good writer...

By sameera khan

Then the r k said, I am a writer …

As it happens in your stories, they both smiled at each other, then they she said lets meet on evinig…

will go from there too then I told him ok I will get ready in the evening r k …

time because I don't like people who lie down and two I made a plan after that they both went their separate ways in the evening

"In the evening, r k…… went to pick up Malini, ………

they both reached a place, as soon as Malini saw this place, she liked it so much   It was just like lying down, then he opened the door

of the car and took her out from there holding her hand and both of them got out of there………

He gave the order for coffee and said to the waiter…

you will always remember this evening,…… then their coffee came and she drank coffee and like it

Ypu like but I didn't make it

  You didn't make it   I know you didn't make it I am giving it You made it Then he told malni…

  I was joking I know who made this coffee Mani asked who made it

Then the rest   He said, "this is by anil

" Malin laughed and said, "No, it is good joke

"It is not good In truth,   it has not been made enough " This is not a joke, this is a fact, it is not advanced enough

"malnl said and this too don't joke the character of the story is in the story so how can it actually happen you didn't make it I know now do anything to impress me said let's press me Not because the narrator has not really made it for you……

She said, "Look, I have come here We will talk here, but if you want to talk about the story now, then I will leave here…

" She said angrily

r k said, "malni don't go

" I am not joking with you   It is really made by Anil   "

"How can the role of a story be in reality?"

He and i   I was a friend and I made the character of this story inspired by my own life…

I know Anil was such a real person   He was my friend   We were very good   But I kill him…,

"O Malni, I was scared, b…

"She fell asleep while the story progressed when she woke up the story was in front of her not all the pages are fill…

then she remembered she has to finish the story then suddenly she got a call she picked up the phone

By sameera khan

"hello ragini how are you what's up…

fraddy…why call What is it,……

she asked ……

Fraddy said   "have been asking whether the story is complete or not   It was also asking by boss……,

then ragni said ……look, I think that the climax of the last part of this story will not be written by me   You must know very well that this book written by Prince sah…

is the last book and its edition is the last and there is no better writer fraddy said…… than you who can write it because you are his daughter and you know more about him That's why I wanted yo…

"Look, fraddy I can't say anything right now...... ,

but Freddie said but Rangani, you are Prince Shah's student,.........

 "Angrily, he came to his cabin and put his bag and said take some time   The boss's mind is not

  Then freddy came from behind and he said, "But Rangani, you were his student and you were five days before him " Before death,

Ragni said.... I will tell you, Prince, do you want to say something,

By sameera khan

Then Ragini said, "I don't know what they wanted to say and what they wanted to explain They have made so many challenge

 in this story and So many stories are left in the middle and one person is there in every story …..

Let me tell you here that world is a great writer who has passed away and he has one of his students, Ragini   Jessie and she has let him complete the unfinished story and he is such a great writer that everyone was waiting for his book but his death happened and now Rangini is taking this story forward that's why   Everyone wants to know about this story what is the story and everyone wants to know what is the story read f…and if you also want then read it…

"Yes but I will say something

fraddy said now Ragini said it was five days ago when I met her I went to hello baba she used to call her teacher papa to her student because he always treated her like a daughter   Hey Ragini, you come, son, sit down, he began to make her sit next to him, then he said, "Look, Rani, as you know, I have always given you a challenge every time, but I want to give you a challenge that the whole world will remember "

Then they challenged me   It is to be brought before the world, to be told what was the truth of it, what was the reality of it and I had finally done it   The story of that means the story of my affairs is also connected in it, but I am telling it so that you all understand how even small things become big in this world   Then the prince said look and ragni you will write this story then I will understand now you take this story and finish it and then Ragini asked what did I do in it, he said in it you have someone's life   I have to write about someone's death   Ragni got scared then I thought that you have always given me a great challenge, but this time you are giving me a challenge, I don't understand anything, so what should I do? I will understand what you will write that you will

say ragni...   Freddie, what should I do, but for a minute, did he suddenly remember something Freddie, you know, in this story, he also mentioned his parents, but why did he mention his parents, Reddy said, maybe they are his love story world   Who do you want to tell then and the person remembers the love story then he remembered that there is a story mentioned in it love you seven time if he looked for the story in which the movie was made and see what the role was   If it is easy for him to write the urban climax, then he told Freddie, Freddy, search for a movie on Google, please, Love you 7 Times, watch this movie, there is a character named anill in this story, and every character is from every story   She is in the role then Freddie searched then he found out that the movie is band tum ragini said is ok but is this story is any there the fraddy said ye this story can be on a old store of dvd ...   lets go there Ragini thought that it might be a good idea, so she left to go to the store where Freddie believed the address   I have been here before, every old movie is here,

they reached this DVD shop, it was outside the border, it was very small, it was in a dilapidated condition   There was a dictionary shop where all kinds of books were available

"He will reach there,

he saw that there was an old man there   He said to the old man that we want a movie called Love You 7 Time   I don't have this movie so He said

 but there are all kinds of movies here then he said yes but I don't have this movie then ragni said you have seen this movie I have seen it many times I have seen it I saw it many times in my childhood, then at night there was a smile on my face and he asked what is the story of this movie that you can tell me,

 then the holy person said, what do you want to ask, ask me what do you want to know about this story   said there was a person named anil in it where can you tell me about him then the old man was surprised and very worried he said I want to know about anil then ragni said…   yes I want to know about the movie

I want to know about please tell me whatever you know, she said, he was like the writer's friend and he was also a friend in this story   anil was always with him and always got a share of his happiness, so the narrator asked, then this movie was done by sister, was there anything bad in it? That's why I heard that because it was based on reality and the reality was malni and

 r   k...   had killed, but no matter how famous they became, Anil was his friend …

"But when the people came to know that his character, who was so liked by the people, was killed by everyone with their own hands, then people made many cases against him and chased him and tried to kill him   This movie has become a lot of controversies and it has become thats why it is banned by r k then Rangani said did he hit with his hands only the old man said I don't know much about it but yes didn't hit Anil   ARK was the one who killed him and I did not know that much

"Then she remembered that one day the prince above had said, Look, I will not live with you many things, I am not your father, but I have always raised you like a daughter Maybe there were many mistakes made by me in the past or many mistakes were made by my parents, so she didn't understand, but now he understood why he had said that in the past had mentioned that maybe his own parents had killed my family, so he kept me as his daughter, then he remembered that once he had also said, "Look, son, what was old is now " It's gone but the truth remains in front of him If someone thinks that I have done something wrong with you, then don't curse me and just think about it It was late at night, friendly   told her that I should go home and you too   Ragni said to fraddy…

"She lived in her house and fell asleep Prince Prince show what happened   Ragini looks very worried   Ragini said I am worried   I don't understand the climax of the story you gave me   There is no story, you know why it has not been discussed that you people will write it, I will read it a lot, you are the problem of the world   We want to know what is your latest story everyone wants to know this story want to spend its edition if I will give any such link then people will spoil the petition for you then he said look and story   Whatever you write, it doesn't matter what impact you leave on the writer's heart, whatever I write, I will like it

he disappears outside and her eyes open

The next day she met fraddy…

Freddy asked her what are you going to do

Ragni said I know what I have to do………

Next seen

"Someone asked Rani, have you written this story from reality or did you just think that you will write it from her then Ragni said I have written this story for my baba, my baba ji   I know everything I wrote for them, now whether you like this story or not, I don't know, but I wrote this story only for them, then someone asked if they gave you any instructions before dying   Before you write this story like this, write it like this then Rangi said yes he said I wrote this story as I left write it like this then Rangi said yes he said I wrote this story as I left it and it should end from where it started and I have tried my best   And what I have written is in front of you   Everyone was celebrating the success of the book that ragni had written, the story of malni Shah and r k also

That movie was still alive in their hearts, but everyone knew the truth, so someone pointed ragni and that point was his friend, he was wearing his watch in his hand, he pointed to the watch, it was time   Come on, then she got up from the press ......

and started to leave from there   In the press there, people asked, "Stop, stop, I want to ask you a question, but she didn't stop and left "

opened the door and said let's go now and they both started leaving there laughing happily after many days so much happiness has come so Ragini told fraddy said yes of course I am getting a lot of happiness too it and it should end from where it started and I have tried my best......

then thet fraddy opened the door of the car, the car was parked in a place where there was a very beautiful beach, there was a house on the beach, there was a table on which the candle lights were burning, everything was very beautiful, then ragny is said to him that I don't intend to propose, then she became different, then he gave her a coffee and a card, when the order came to her, the water give a card with coffe to ragni…… Then Ragini opened the card and saw it She was shocked and worried until she was very scared

It was written in it Dear, I am your dear I am here to enjoy this coffee because I made it Know Me Very Well Remember Me……

The end

…………

www.ingramcontent.com/pod-product-compliance
Lightning Source LLC
Chambersburg PA
CBHW031328250726
48656CB00005B/2024